Narrative in Landscape

Ireland Young

BookLeaf Publishing

India | USA | UK

Presentation by *BookLeaf Publishing*

Web: www.bookleafpub.com

E-mail: info@bookleafpub.com

ISBN: 9789360940591

First edition 2024

To my family, my friends, my mentors, and the Earth.

ACKNOWLEDGEMENT

There are so many who have contributed to this book. First, I could not have done it without Lydia, my big sister in all but blood, lifelong outing buddy, and the one who introduced me to #TheWriteAngle in the first place. I would also like to thank my family, who have cheered me on for the past two decades. Mom, Dad, you have been my go-to editors since I brought home my first essay. You always knew how to walk me through each sentence and make it pack a punch. Molly, John, Charlie, Eileen, and Gugu, thank you for taking care of me during our trip to Ireland in June of 2023. And thank you to my actual sisters, Ronan and Addie, for always listening to my three-hour brain rots about made-up fantasy worlds. And I cannot forget you, Nonnie. Thank you for showing me the magic of walking in the woods and listening to the birds.

I am also eternally grateful for the friends who have been with me through thick and thin. Sarah, you have looked out for me since 7th grade. Even when I had to transfer schools, you were always there for me, whether it was to discuss our favorite anime, share book ideas, or go on long walks. I also want to thank Kieran, who reached out to me in 2022 to rebuild our childhood friendship, and with whom I have treasured memories of playing in the woods and drawing giant fantasy maps. And a big thanks to Sander, Roz, Eleanor, Megan, Talia, Ollie, Cameron, and Xi. Without your constant support, openness, and authenticity, I would not be where I am today.

To everyone on the Write Here, Write Now Board of 2023-2024, thank you for getting me out of bed, into a chair, and tapping on my keyboard every day. Specifically, Eva, our superb and confident co-president; Liv and Kaylee, our bold and brilliant events coordinators; Antara, our suave and splendid treasurer; Ev and Nina, our slick and savvy audio/visual managers; Emma and Melanie, our publicists/conductors of digital chaos; and Quinn, our dastardly and diligent secretary. I would also like to thank Gale, our former publicist/Overlord of Digital Chaos who continues to inspire me with absurd ideas, and Lauren, our former co-president who introduced me to anti-racism, and taught me how to lead a college writing club.

I would also like to extend a big thank you to the counselors and campers of Pok-O-MacCready who inspired my six-year journey up the Adirondack High Peaks. Jacob Gittler, Hannah Bronstein, Peter "Smitty" Myers, Sarah "Smacky" Mackay, Sean Green, and Driver Mac, you showed me how to have fun when the journey sucked. I owe my love of hardcore hiking, alpine zones, mud, and instant oatmeal to you. And thank you Nora, Sam, Ronan, Addie, Ruby, Ben, Nathalia, Prisca, Grace, Ella, and Sage for dressing up in goofy superhero costumes and seeing me through on my last 46er. Finally, without Dena, I would have never considered going to summer camp in the first place. I hope that, even though I am older now, we can still connect over our love of camp and creative writing.

Although this book is not for any class, it would have been impossible to write without the many mentors I had the privilege to meet in middle school, high school, and college. I would like to thank Mr. Slater, my 7th grade science teacher who filled lunchtimes with Mythbusters, and class time with introductory biology, physics, chemistry, electromagnetism, and quantum theory. I would also like to thank Mrs. Sears, my 7th grade English teacher who, through fun units and excellent feedback, made me fall in love with writing for the very first time.

I would be remiss if I did not acknowledge the massive contributions of my teachers at Vermont Commons School, so I would like to thank Mark Cline Lucey, my 10th-12th grade history teacher, for teaching me how to debate, write about history, and survive a five-day hiking trip in the middle of winter. I would also like to thank Jennifer Cohen, my 10th-12th grade English teacher, for teaching me how to write memoirs, and for accepting me when I first came out as aromantic and asexual.

I also need to give a huge thanks to my professors and educators in the Biology and Earth Science Departments at Mount Holyoke College. To Amy Frary, who introduced me to plant biology, Gretchen Peltier, who taught me about environmental and public health, and Sarah Bacon, who left me forever starstruck by cephalopods and bumblebees. To the marvelous Kate Ballantine, who rekindled my love of environmental science and gave me the technical skills needed to monitor forest, water, and soil quality. And to Professor Corson, Sylvia Cifuentes, and Kevin Surprise, who introduced me to the complex realms of climate change, environmental racism, racial capitalism, political geography, political ecology, colonialism, indigenous knowledges, and indigenous politics. All of you have me hopeful for a future of restorative pluriverses.

And a special, special thanks to Lauret Savoy and Timothy Farnham. I signed up for ENVST-333: Narrative and Landscape at the very last minute, and it was one of the best decisions I have ever made. Plus, out of all the people who have guided me, you have had the most profound impact on the contents of this book.

Hats off to all of you, you amazing humans! And lastly, thank you BookLeaf Publishing for reading, arranging, and publishing my amateur work. I hope this adventure was as amazing for you as it was for me.

PREFACE

Creative writing is hard. Very hard.

As a kid, I was famous for stapling heaps of paper into "books" and only illustrating the first two or so pages. As a teenager, I became more entranced by the idea of writing than the physical act, so I watched thousands of YouTube videos on writing and created only a handful of half-baked stories. It was also around this time I grew perfectionistic, and used academic achievement to distract myself from dwindling friendships.

Productivity. Procrastination. Perfectionism. I could cry rivers about this unholy trinity, but here is the crazy part: After 21 years of wallowing in writerly limbo, I wrote my first book in 21 days.

I am still in shock. A product of BookLeaf Publishing's annual writing challenge, #TheWriteAngle, Narrative in Landscape contains 21 poems I wrote between December 21, 2023, and January 10, 2024. Each is inspired by one video and four creative essays I submitted for a college seminar called

ENVST-333: Narrative and Landscape. Taught by professors Lauret Savoy and Tim Farnham, this class met every Thursday for several months to explore the links between narrative and land. Our topics ranged from Lauret's Trace: Memory, History, Race and the American Landscape to our own familial environmental histories. 'Hard residues,' Lauret called them, both in class and in Trace. Through each project, I learned how to build bridges over the societal fault lines dividing land, life, environment, history, family, memory, climate change, capitalism, race, colonialism, racism, privilege, humanity, more-than-humans, alienation, belonging, health, death, identity, war, love, hate, and forgiveness. Bridging the gaps between these domains rather than exploring them in isolation has been crucial for helping me navigate my own landscapes, and even start healing some old wounds.

And what better way to investigate these connections further than with poetry? Something people have been using for navigation and healing for thousands of years?

This book is a testament to myself and other aspiring writers. Writing 21 poems after learning about #TheWriteAngle three days before it began was challenging, but provided clear expectations, set up, and payoff. Narrative in Landscape is proof that writers of any age, genre, identity, experience, and skill can write in spite of and to spite productivity, procrastination, and perfectionism. Felicia Rose Chavez in her 2021 The Anti-Racist Writing Workshop says it best: "But I will write anyway." To me, every time we write anyway, we actively engage with the hard residue of writing itself.

And that makes you courageous.

A perfect land

A perfect land is one pristine
Rich in beauty and light
A perfect land is untouched and free
Its exploration human birthright
Caverns veined with gems and gold
Jungles savaging with life
Bogs exhaling noxious mist
Meadows a-hum and bright
The stories chime a million times
From movies, mouth, and books
"This land is your land!"
Perfection! No need for second looks.

Yeah. Perfection.
I pause a nature documentary on a computer
forged from butchered underlands and bleeding
fingers
Open a book about elves and dragons wrought
from the bones of a forest on indigenous soil
Eat corn chips processed from gaunt croplands
and back-broke migrant workers

Yeah.
No need for second looks.

Return to the origins

What is land?
Some would consult dictionaries, others their
phones
point toward a painting, or step out the door
Each meaning given a grasp given form
Through writing, pixel, brushstroke, and
movement
Does that make land a dictionary? A phone? A
painting? A threshold?
This line of text that's eight words long?

Each meaning given speaks of the limits of
definition and language
How they draw the border between is and isn't
and scramble up branches of iteration
What is land?
Each meaning given feels like it takes
land farther away from its origins

So maybe we should return to an origin
maybe Earth

Feel the star-swirled earthpressure grip your
feet,

the lightstorm of photons shattering across your
retinas,
the quantumquakes of quantumlands rapping
your eardrums,
the chemical dance of spit, snot, and airflow
through sinus and tongue

Take it out.

Messy, touched, plural

What is land?
What is it to you?

About eight

Hiking.
Fucking hiking.
I yank my shoelaces tight beneath an indigo sky
Twelve of us bubbly, one of us burst
One puking breakfast on the gravel behind
I find her penning something at the trailhead
How long's the trip?
"About eight" she shuts the log

Huff and puff
Under branches, over streams
Knotted and frayed in a hellish weave
I'm dragged by future friends; the needles
Up, up up—
Down. A lichened rock rips my knee.
She calls from behind: "Hurry, let's go go go!"
How much longer?
"About eight!" She said

Climb, climb
Climb, climb until muscles burst
And shoulder straps bite
Now above the pines
Where sun dries sweat on brows,
resin plugs the nose,

And ruffled granite strikes my heel.
Hand on knee, I hiss and see
The backs of crows on thermals
Mountain wind fluting through hollow
trunks and valleys

She calls from up front: "C'mon c'mon, we're
almost there!"
Where?
"About eight!" She points ahead

Sphagnum moss

Stringy-green, and tucked in the shademarsh
clumps
Beside hornworts, fungi, and bryophytes
soaked with water twenty-times your own
weight
so that you stream like a sponge when pressed

You cover one percent of all the Earth
After eons of inch and creep
I can't believe you've been sinking carbon
Since before the first Carboniferous body sank

You are hundreds among millions
Peripheral in sight and mind
That deserves a standing ovation
For all that you've done so far

Reality, unreality

Reality, unreality
Pushing culture, story, creation
Destruction, erasure, hate
Overwriting each other on mind and land
Layering/effacing, penning/erasing,
Speaking/hushing, drying/gushing
Spitting/cracking, seedling/sapling
Cycles in movement, cycles in still
Cycled by humans, more-thans, more
Racism. Sexism. Hatred. War.
Bloodshed. Cruelty. Lies
kill
Kill
Kill kill
Kill kill kill kill
Kill kill kill kill kill kill kill kill kill
Killuw!uie#wmrji2!@7qo%mje2[qhjv&b*kjTln
kHlkcl;ltJxtxCFTYU—

What lies behind your dream?
American? Capital? Greed?
How much do you know?
Not know?
Un-know?
Known?

Reality. Unreality.
Here. I'm here!
Hold on!
I've got you.
I've got you.

Just breathe..

Ireland, like the country

"I'm Ireland, like the country" is how I greet
most strangers
"You've got the hair and freckles!" They laugh
"Are you actually Irish?"
"Are you lucky?"
"A leprechaun?"
"A drinker?"
"Fiery?"

Am I Irish? No
I'm Irish, German, hiking, writing, indecisive,
snake-loving, slightly overweight, walking,
talking, and breathing all at once.
Am I lucky? No
I'm White, so the system looks me over with
averted eyes.
Am I a leprechaun? No
my family has had the privilege to work hard for
their small pot of gold.
Am I a drinker? No
But I hope you have access to clean water too.
Am I fiery? Yeah
no thanks to myself and you

802

A state you forget and a land you remember
On autumnal postcards you buy from the
country store on your way to Canada
One area, one code, where the ivory towers
pierce the horizon
from college and colonial-style towns
resting on marbled bedrock that folds the earth
into knotted spines and hollows; the Green
Mountain State
Lies low enough to let you settle, and high
enough to trip the truth
of how the Valley pumps the world's mess and
muddle
down slithering sap line into cold gray buckets
to be sugar-shackled up until it's boiled down
into syrup
that's easier to swallow

your Wild

You want to make the world Wild again
"Reduce, reuse, recycle!" you shout
As they ship your broken glass overseas
to be burned and buried with the other trash
You want to make the world Wild again
"Save the polar bears, wolves, and jungles!" you
cry
While you stomp snakes, spray the grass, and
flush
spiders down the toilet
You want to make the world Wild again
"Go solar, electric, nuclear!" you weep
As they wash away your green with hybrids,
price tags, and
ethics slicked with oil and blood
You want to make the world Wild again
But how much of the Wild is
Grown from Hollywood sets
seeded by science and data
grown by state and policy
seeded by greed and industry
Grown by silencing, omitting, and colonizing
indigenous wisdom, knowledges, and people?

How much of the Wild is real
and how much of it is myth?

Landlocked

A year ago, I was the only Ireland
Mom, Dad, sisters, grandparents
All roosting on the same road
Until we packed our backs and flew the coop
across the Atlantic

People say your family's roots run deep, but for
me, it's like they fly
Like how Dad's side migrated from the Emerald
Isle and beyond
to spread their wings across the North American
continent
Bus drivers in Greensboro, profs in the
Chesapeake, ranchers out in Lusk
Until Dr. Mom and Dr. Dad came and moved us
to Vermont
Locking me and my sisters in a beautiful cage
That shut out the others' calls

Gugu

My Great Aunt came with us to Ireland last
summer
For three weeks, her stories lit the pubs and
brimmed with crow-footed smiles and
ravenlaughs.
Me the awestruck, she the storyteller.

She and her mother left when the Troubles were
brewing.
For three weeks, we traced the bakeries,
churches, and murals of her youth.
Me who waved hello, she who waved goodbye.

In Virginia, she was baptized a nun, then a
secretary before retiring to the suburbs.
For three weeks, she led us through streets while
I led her over curbs.
My first visit; her, her last.

Catholicism, Second-Wave feminism, and
sheltered living embroider her like ivy on ruins.
Vibrant and loving you, abrasive and judging
you
quicker than Christ on coffee

For three weeks she wore the same gray shirt
patterned with blue anchors. It was made of
thick cloth, but when going to steady her
forearm, my fingers would catch on its nicks and
tears.
I always meant to ask her where she got it.

Ireland greets you

Shop bells tinkle, wooden signs creak
Mary puts on the kettle, and brushes her thumb
across my forehead,
murmuring
Holy water drips down
I want to meet everyone here and hear their story
Because Ireland greets you like a friend,
Even when you can't stay long

A sharp right rustles the pamphlets in the cup
holder
Sheep-flecked hills through rain-flecked glass
Hills and forests rippling mountainward like a
quilt mid-flourish
I want to break out and sprint forever
Because Ireland runs beside you fervently and
verdantly
While the family stick shift stalls on two-lane
roads built for one

Knocktopher. Kilkenny. Maghera.
Behind each ridge, castles hail the stormy sun
Cappoquin. Derry. Dublin.
Behind each castle, towns trail oldpenny street
through shanty

Jerpoint. Donegal. The River Nore.
Behind each town, churches grail the pews with
gemlight
Although I don't believe, I do believe
My world just got bigger
Because Ireland confides in you a history rich as
any
Brewed in ale and bog

But the family can't wait— the kettle boils

Pangaean bedrock

The Giant's Causeway churns skyward like a
black basalt honeycomb
Spitting salt and brine
The Carrick-A-Rede snaps taut beneath breeze
and boot
Above silent waves
The Rock of Cashel guards the jackdaws of
Tipperary
despite the millennium's pickaxe

Ireland invites me to where history lies wounded
yet strong
Scarred by Vikings, scabbed over by keeps
Christened by saints and crucified by kings
Illuminated by manuscripts, torched by
Cromwell
Blistered by blight and religious divide
Troubled by the Troubles and Brexit's collide
Yet, on shaking legs, still standing
Because Ireland carries the strength of Brigid
and Cú Chulainn
and resilience of Pangaean bedrock

I'm sitting in a pub.

Ale upon laughter, chips on checkered wax
paper, grease on stamped silverware
Dad signs the check. I think about Pangaea
Once one
scattered by geology and names like 'Ireland'
and 'US'

We leave tomorrow

From small moments

It was during the last few days when Dad's side
closened
And connections budded from small moments
Giles and Goldie grazing my knuckles after
learning how to fist-bump
Joe and I shaking on our Cúl Hero card
exchange
My cousins assuring me that atheists can't
condemn innocent souls by screwing up mass
Jolene accusing "horseback riding" of being
redundant
My aunt cursing and swerving the car between a
hundred tractors and a hundred-foot drop
Mom and Dad singing and dancing after
reception and wine
One sister picking glass off the ground, one
sister with Nonnie watching sea shanties weep
My middle sister tossing a glass bottle on the
pavement for the hell of it
Small moments that fly away if unnoticed, but
stick when remembered
like sweet pollen from blossoms

Blueberries dropped in milk

You said I was quiet when born
Bald and owl-blinking with eyes like blueberries
dropped in milk
I don't remember North Carolina, but I
remember Maine
and that big yellow house on Stevens Avenue
With its chickadees and rain
and sidewalks shaggy with pinecones
Playing fetch with the dogs in Baxter Woods
Feeding ducks in the graveyard pond
Eating sand with a shovel like Little Miss Muffet
and a teacher slapping the bucket away...
Then that big white house on Cider Mill Road
I don't remember being six; only wiping my
crusties in the blink of knobs and vanity mirrors
of the minivan juddering over Vermont
pavement
Purple bruises, yellow bus, blue birthday
Dad unscrewing my training wheels, Mom
building a ramp for her ailing Beecher
garter snakes peering from slate stone wall

In the middle of the yard, a marble square with a
circle window
stood in the grass like a lonely door

Edges softened in the bubble glass pane
It's too heavy to open
And also probably leads nowhere

Mom & Dad

She saws wood in the garage, he saws wood on
the pillow
She can't sleep without socks, he'll take shorts
over pants
She leaves her chewed-up gum on cup lids and
dashboards
He leaves his pens exploded in the couches and
mugs
She prefers rom-coms to his All Elite Wrestling
He would prefer the kitchen emptied of her
chocolate and chips
She builds barns, he feeds chickens and sheep
She works the night shift, he cooks our dinner
She likes his waffles while he likes her banana
bread
She taught me writing while he taught me math
She sets up the plans while he sets up Catan
She mends broken bodies, he, the silence

She gives, he gives
She cares, he cares
Quiet yet devoted
Making and mending
Mending and making
For 22 years

I love you
Ah-boo

Found when lost

Whether it's warm or cold, humid or dry
Nonnie will take me to hear the bobolinks or ski
along the herd paths
Where time evaporates like lake-fog beneath a
smiling sun
Whether cloistered by summerglade hardwoods
or swaddled in snowy thickets
Nonnie will always find a way, usually to laugh
at how badly we followed the map
And her laugh is my favorite

Sisters

I used to pull your hair hard enough to make you
scream
and wish you could curse like Dad when he
stubs his toe… or Mom when she stubs her's
I'd yell at you, spit on you, fart on you
Steal your Polly Pockets, eat the last muffin, and
break all your Legos
I would also try to be better than you at
everything
Me, the haughty brown-nosing fool
You, the stubborn singing cynic
You, the surly punk violinist
We'd turn the house into a battleground for
pointless fights
And throw shit on the floor for Mom and Dad to
clean or stub more toes on

How the hell are you my friends today?

Interims, home

Once I walked to tune the world out
Walked with the dogs and land behind our
house:
A crunching dirt road shouldered by field and
forest that shivered
with rose gold dusks, fireleaf play, and roughgrit
snow
Here and there, it's startled by a pond, an apple
tree, or pipe
To me, this land is the rambling interim between
house and home
where I feel safe and held
While I can't speak for the dogs, I know it
makes them happy too
Before us, however, this land was part of the
ancestral home
of the Wabanaki, Abenaki, and Mohican
peoples.
A home with histories, love, and knowledge
entwining like arms of a river

A home.
So much more than a safe and happy space.

Now I walk to remember

Though I can never be the voices or memories
of the people and land before

Her father

She gives her heart; her father, his ego
Shackles you down with your own guilt and
good grace
Fresh wood for his rotting podium
She begged her mother to divorce
Everything spent on handshakes and
supplements
Everything a scam, demand, or a crash that's
still burning
Her mother is still with him
Tripping over his purchases in the hallway
She wonders why he cheats them all and cheats
the law
Made her roll it all up
until the black helicopters descended upon the
garden like crows to roadkill

He's falling more, now, or perhaps the ditches
are deepening
She'd better fix that damn paint job soon, he
says
On the garage she built for him

His loneliness hangs like the beer on his breath

So I kept him company until he taught me what
his words could not
Bent myself backward when hugging to conform
to the crook of his spine
Mangled and fused in place by a spell of failed
back surgeries
But he never listened
Never considered
He might be a veteran, but he'll never be the
expert on her

..

stop..

.

.

..

..

-

.

STOP

Swing Set

Mom built us an outdoor swing set years ago
It can seat three, but I'm the only one who visits
Usually when I'm restless and the mindlands are
on fire
I lean back and kick off the earth to float with
the sky, star, and voidlands
sometimes playing, sometimes grieving
sometimes angry, sometimes thinking
A pondering wandering path
in my home on the swings that bridge Earth with
all lands

9 789360 940591